# Theme Park Insider
# Visits
# The Wizarding World
# of Harry Potter

ROBERT NILES

# CONTENTS

*Hogwarts Castle at The Wizarding World of Harry Potter — Hogsmeade at Universal's Islands of Adventure theme park in Orlando, Florida.*

# INTRODUCTION AND HISTORY OF UNIVERSAL'S WIZARDING WORLD

J.K. Rowling's Harry Potter series has earned more money than any entertainment franchise in history — topping the box office charts with more than two billion dollars in ticket sales, and the best-seller lists with nearly half a billion books sold. No wonder that so many top theme park companies wanted to bring Rowling's "wizarding world" to their parks.

Warner Bros. bought the film and merchandising rights to Harry Potter in 1999. But Warner Bros. does not own a major theme park chain, so rival studios Disney and Universal — which do own and run parks — both made efforts to acquire the theme park rights from Rowling and Warner Bros. Walt Disney Imagineering and Universal Creative — the theme park design divisions of each company, respectively — created plans for Harry Potter-themed attractions and presented them to Rowling and others involved in the negotiations. Many theme park fans assumed that Disney, as the market leader in theme parks and being so well-known for creating entertainment aimed at children, would win the rights. But, ultimately, Universal prevailed. On May 31, 2007, Universal and Warner Bros. announced that The Wizarding World of Harry Potter would come to the Universal Orlando Resort.

But Universal wouldn't be building The Wizarding World from scratch. Instead, the company decided that it would transform a portion of The Lost Continent land at its Islands of Adventure theme park in Orlando into the new Harry Potter land. The Lost Continent featured attractions based on old European mythology, including dragons, unicorns and other magical creatures also found in the Harry Potter books. So it wasn't too much of a stretch to convert some of those existing locations over to the new Harry Potter theme.

Universal would keep two roller coasters from The Lost Continent and rename them for The Wizarding World of Harry Potter. Dueling Dragons, an inverted roller coaster from Swiss manufacturer Bolliger & Mabillard, would become "Dragon Challenge," themed to the Triwizard Tournament from *Harry Potter and the Goblet of Fire*. And The Flying Unicorn, a junior coaster from Vekoma, would become "The Flying Hippogriff," with a recreation of Hagrid's hut to be added within the footprint of the coaster's track.

Construction began in early 2008. Although Universal would keep the two coasters, as well as some of the underlying infrastructure in the area, The Wizarding World would end up looking very different than the old Lost Continent land. The Wizarding World would recreate the village of Hogsmeade from the Harry Potter books and films, with snow-capped shops and restaurant lining the main street, leading up to Hogwarts Castle.

The castle itself would be built in a "forced perspective" style that would create a visual illusion of a full-sized, magical Scottish castle rising above an Orlando theme park. Force perspective buildings start at "normal" size on their ground floors, with each additional upper floor built to smaller and smaller scale, mimicking the way that things far away look smaller to the eye. (Disney uses this same technique for its theme park castles.)

Inside Hogwarts, visitors would find an attraction within an attraction, as the queue for the ride within the castle would take visitors through a walking tour of some of the famous sights within the Hogwarts School of Witchcraft and Wizardry, including the Mirror of Erised, Dumbledore's office, the Defense Against Dark Arts classroom, and the Gryffindor common room.

But the highlight of the entire land would be the ride inside Hogwarts Castle, featuring a revolutionary new ride system that would place visitors in seats mounted on rotating robot arms, which would then carry visitors through an adventure with Harry and his friends.

The Wizarding World of Harry Potter at Universal Orlando's Islands of Adventure theme park opened officially to the public on Friday, June 18, 2010. The public opening came at the end of a three-day media event, which saw J.K. Rowling and Harry Potter stars Daniel Radcliffe [Harry Potter], Rupert Grint [Ron Weasley], Tom Felton [Draco Malfoy], Michael Gambon [Albus Dumbledore], Matthew Lewis [Neville Longbottom], James Phelps [Fred Weasley], Oliver Phelps [George Weasley], Bonnie Wright [Ginny Weasley], and Warwick Davis [Griphook / Professor Filius Flitwick] visit the new land for a sneak peek, with all but Rowling meeting the assembled press. (We will hear from many of these stars later in the book.)

On the day of the official opening, visitors started arriving at Universal Orlando in the middle of the night, crowding the freeway overpass leading into the resort's parking garages even before they opened for the day. By the time of the opening ceremony in the morning, the line to get into the new land extended all the way around the park and into and through the adjacent CityWalk dining and shopping area. Estimates put the length of the line at more than half a mile, and fans near the back of the line reported waiting more than eight hours just to get into the new land.

The Wizarding World of Harry Potter pushed Islands of Adventure to a stunning 30.2% increase in attendance in its first year. (Remember that the land was open only for the second half of the year.) Islands of Adventure posted an additional 29% attendance jump on top of that in 2011, the first full year of operation for The Wizarding World. With attendance soaring — and revenue and profits along with it — Universal moved quickly to expand The Wizarding World. Since then, Universal Parks & Resorts has announced plans to expand The Wizarding World of Harry Potter to three other Universal theme parks: Universal Studios Florida, Universal Studios Japan, and Universal Studios Hollywood. That leaves Universal Studios Singapore as the only current Universal theme park without a Harry Potter land open or under construction.

Of course, old perceptions die hard. On the day of The Wizarding World's opening, CBS posted a story on its website about the new Harry Potter land "at Walt Disney World." Many Orlando visitors continue be surprised that they need a Universal ticket to see the Wizarding World, and that Potter isn't part of the Walt Disney World empire.

In this guide, we will describe the rides, shows, restaurants and shops to be found in The Wizarding World of Harry Potter — Hogsmeade, as well as those found in Universal Orlando's second Wizarding World, The Wizarding World of Harry Potter — Diagon Alley, which opened in neighboring Universal Studios Florida in the summer of 2014. We will offer tips on planning a visit to the Universal Orlando Resort, based on the experience of thousands of ThemeParkInsider.com readers who have visited the lands since their opening. We also will tell you about the Wizarding Worlds in Japan and in Hollywood, and hear from some of the creative leaders who helped design and build these lands. Finally, we'll also hear from the stars of the Harry Potter films, who will talk about their reactions to walking into these "real life" Wizarding Worlds for the first time.

*The view down the Hogsmeade high street at Universal's Islands of Adventure.*

# THE WIZARDING WORLD OF HARRY POTTER — HOGSMEADE

The original Wizarding World soft-opened in late May 2010, following the 2007 announcement that Universal had secured the theme park rights to J.K. Rowling's characters and would be bringing them to the Universal Orlando Resort. Themed to the village of Hogsmeade from the Harry Potter books and films, the original Wizarding World land was designed by Universal Creative in consultation with author J.K. Rowling and Harry Potter film production designer Stuart Craig. It included one new attraction, "Harry Potter and the Forbidden Journey," as well as two re-themed rides, plus multiple shops and a restaurant.

Located in the rear of the Islands of Adventure theme park, The Wizarding World of Harry Potter — Hogsmeade can be approached from two directions. The "back way" takes you clock-wise around the park's central lagoon, bringing you into The Wizarding World from the park's Jurassic Park land. But the more visually impressive approach is to enter from what remains of The Lost Continent, following the park's central lagoon in a counter-clockwise direction from the entrance. This places you at the very end of the Hogsmeade "high street," allowing you a wonderful visual "reveal" of the Hogwarts Castle as you walk down the street of snow-capped storefronts, many adorned with animated and sometimes even interactive windows.

With the opening of The Wizarding World of Harry Potter — Diagon Alley in Universal Studios Florida, there's now a third way to enter Hogsmeade Village — by taking a trip on the Hogwarts Express. We will talk more about that experience, in a bit.

But for now, let's offer our description of Hogsmeade, and everything to be found within it. Because we can't bear to save the best for last, let's start with a description and our review of the land's signature attraction, the one inside Hogwarts Castle.

## Harry Potter and the Forbidden Journey

*Theme Park Insider readers' rating:* 9/10 (Outstanding)
*Minimum height to ride: 48 inches*

The signature attraction in the Wizarding World of Harry Potter at Universal's Islands of Adventure theme park is "Harry Potter and the Forbidden Journey," a twisting, tilting dark ride through and around Hogwarts Castle.

The first sign of a good theme park ride is that there is no sign. As you walk up to the entrance, you're not approaching another attraction in a theme park — you really feel like you are walking up to Hogwarts Castle. Working with the design team from the Harry Potter films, Universal Creative has developed an edifice that surpasses even Disney's Cinderella's Castle for scale and visual detail. Expect to dodge crowds of fans queuing not for the ride, but to take pictures in front of what surely will become one of the Orlando area's best photo ops.

The story behind all of this is that Headmaster Albus Dumbledore has opened the Hogwarts School of Witchcraft and Wizardry to Muggle tours for the first time, to the disgust of Salazar Slytherin, who'll let you know that in the castle's Portrait Hall.

Yes, the portraits in the hall, which you will see in the queue of the ride, really do move and speak to another, just as in the films, in an effect that is completely believable.

You might have seen attempts at moving portraits in theme parks before. The Wizarding World has several others throughout the land, relying (as is typical for this sort of thing) on video screens. But the portraits within the castle don't look like TV screens embedded in a frame. They look like moving paintings — as simple and profound as that sounds.

The queue for the ride consists of a walking tour through the Hogwarts Castle, starting in the dungeons, then continuing through the Herbology greenhouse, the Gryffindor common room and other sites. The walk-through would merit a recommendation on its own, but as a pre-show for a ride? Incredible. Universal Creative sets expectations almost impossibly high in this queue, with elaborately detailed recreations of Dumbledore's office and the Defense Against the Dark Arts Classroom, enhanced with filmed appearances from Daniel Radcliffe, Rupert Grint, Emma Watson, and Michael Gambon, reprising their roles as Harry, Ron, Hermione, and Dumbledore.

The Hogwarts headmaster has arranged for Professor Binns to present a lecture "of just a few hours" on Hogwarts' history, but Harry and his friends arrive in the classroom to rescue us from that deadly boring fate. Instead, we're off to the Room of Requirement, where Hermione will enchant a bench for us to ride on, then send us into the Floo Network to whisk us on our way, once we're seated and our over-the-shoulder harnesses are snapped into place.

As the ride gets going, we end up at the top of the Astronomy tower, where we're to follow Harry and Ron, on their broomsticks, over to the Quidditch pitch. But, as always on theme park rides, something goes terribly wrong. A dragon appears, setting up the ride's first stunning encounter with an animatronic figure, as we come face-to-face with the beast.

Forbidden Journey employs a first-of-its-kind ride system, involving bench seats mounted on the end of Kuka robot arms that each travel on a track through the ride building. At times, we're traveling in tandem with curved screens that accommodate super-sharp, high-definition projection, allowing us personal moments with the Harry Potter characters. At other times, the screens disappear and we're traveling through large, open practical sets, with animatronics and multiple theatrical effects immersing us in the broader scale of Hogwarts and the Forbidden Forest.

Imagine an Omnimover dark ride, such as Disney's Haunted Mansion. But instead of riding in cars that move only in one dimension, rotating on a stable axis, our robot arms rotate and elevate along three axes — left and right, up and down, and tilting diagonally — as they carry us through the show environment.

Creative director Thierry Coup has surpassed his work on Universal's Amazing Adventures of Spider-Man with Forbidden Journey. Together, the ride and show elements deliver several of the most dynamic, iconic moments from the Harry Potter series, while placing you into that action. You will face that dragon, along with massive spiders and Dementors, on the most action-packed day of hooky since *Ferris Bueller's Day Off.*

Eventually, of course, the wizards save the day and everyone exits happily into the gift shop. After 10 years, we, at last, have a ride that exceeds Spider-Man, a rousing journey through an iconic pop-culture franchise that thrills riders with unique experiences at every turn.

When the media complain about kids' short attention spans these days, I laugh. Kids who queue up at midnight to buy and read 750-page books straight through, as they did with the release of the later Potter books, do not lack the ability to pay attention. J.K. Rowling's creation inspired a generation of children (and many adults) to embrace literature. And now it's inspired a creative team to build the most advanced and engaging attraction in theme park industry history.

Forget fairies or wizards. *That* is magic.

## Dragon Challenge

*Theme Park Insider readers' rating:* 8/10 (Commendable)
*Minimum height to ride: 54 inches*

While "Harry Potter and the Forbidden Journey" offers a unique ride system through an iconic environment, "Dragon Challenge" offers a Bolliger & Mabillard inverted coaster much like those you could find in more than two dozen other theme and amusement parks through the United States and Europe. And yet, none of those other roller coasters offers as richly detailed a queue and environment as you will find on "Dragon Challenge."

It's the time of the Triwizard Tournament, and you're in the competition. You'll face a choice of riding a Chinese Fireball or a Hungarian Horntail, two dragons that have been selected for this event. As you walk through the elaborate queue, you'll see Arthur Weasley's wrecked Ford Anglia from *Harry Potter and the Chamber of Secrets*, the Champions' Tent, and the Triwizard Cup. Consider riding at night, when your eyes are accustomed to dimmer light, allowing you to better see the elaborately detailed tapestries in the later sections of the queue.

Just before you board, it's time to choose: the Fireball to the left, or the Horntail to the right. These aren't actually "dragons"; they're just the names for the two intertwining roller coaster tracks on the ride. The two tracks are similar, but not identical. They're each 3,200 feet long, with a top height of 125 feet. You'll be on board for 2 minutes and 25 seconds, although that includes the time climbing the hill and a short wait to return to the station to unload. The differences? The Fireball's a bit faster — with the top speed of 65 miles per hour, to the Horntail's 55 mph. The Fireball drops 115 feet from the lift hill, while the Horntail drops (only?) 95 feet. Both tracks include a loop and corkscrews, but the Fireball also includes Immelmann loops (a half-loop with a half-twist that curves out in the opposite direction from where you came into the loop), while the Horntail offers a zero-G roll and a Cobra roll (a half-loop, corkscrew, and half-loop that together look like the hood around the head of a cobra).

Needless to say, these are intense rides, made even more so by the inverted construction. In the roller coaster world, an "inverted" coaster is one where the cars run underneath the track. (Think of a ski lift, only much, much wilder and faster.) With the track above you, instead of underneath as on a traditional coaster, the forces you feel while riding are distributed differently, making inverted coasters feel more intense to many riders than more traditional models feel. In addition, visibility is often more limited in all but the front row, creating a feeling that you are "riding blind," robbing your eyes of the ability to help you anticipate the next move on the track, further amplifying the intensity.

For all these reasons, dedicated coaster fans adore the best inverted models, but casual fans should be warned that these aren't coasters for beginners. That's why "Dragon Challenge" consistently offers the shortest wait of all the attractions in the Wizarding World.

If you visited Islands of Adventure before 2010, you might remember these coasters as "Dueling Dragons," with the Fireball and Horntail named "Fire" and "Ice" back then. The queue was the dragons' ruined-castle lair, and the trains on the two tracks were timed so that they "dueled," with the trains passing close to each other for "near misses" throughout the ride.

Reckless visitors who didn't heed warnings to stow their belongings in lockers caused Universal eventually to change the trains' timing, eliminating the dueling feature, due to several incidents where belongings flew off one train and nearly hit people on the other. So allow us a moment now to implore you to please follow all posted and announced safety rules when you are visiting a theme park. Not only will doing so help keep you safe, your cooperation will help everyone to continue to enjoy these kinds of special experiences. Thank you!

## Flight of the Hippogriff

*Theme Park Insider readers' rating: 7/10 (Good)*
*Minimum height to ride: 36 inches*

"Dragon Challenge" sound like too much for you? Then head over to "Flight of the Hippogriff," a Vekoma junior coaster that offers more kid-sized thrills. At a top speed of just 28 miles per hour, and less than a minute of ride time over a 1,000-foot track, this a great starter coaster for young roller coaster fans-in-training — or for parents and grandparents who've retired from the really wild rides. (If you are visiting or have visited other theme parks in Central Florida, the "Barnstormer" coaster in Walt Disney World's Magic Kingdom is the same Vekoma model as "Flight of the Hippogriff," as is the "Dragon" coaster at Legoland Florida.)

The backstory is that you're here for a Care of Magical Creatures class and will pass Hagrid's hut on your way through the queue. After boarding, you'll come face-to-face with Buckbeak the Hippogriff as you pull away from the station. Be sure to nod your head to earn the beast's respect, then get ready for your ride among the treetops of the Wizarding World, inspired by Harry's ride on Buckbeak in *Harry Potter and the Prisoner of Azkaban*.

## Hogwarts Express: Hogsmeade to London

*Theme Park Insider readers' rating: 9/10 (Outstanding)*
*No minimum height to ride*

Hogsmeade's Hogwarts Express station opened in July 2014, with the debut of The Wizarding World of Harry Potter — Diagon Alley in neighboring Universal Studios Florida. The Hogwarts Express connects the two Wizarding Worlds in the two parks, so you must have a Universal

Orlando "Park to Park" ticket to board the ride. You will disembark over in Universal Studios Florida after you ride, so make sure that you're ready to move over to the other park before you board.

We will write more about Hogwarts Express in the Diagon Alley section of this guide, but let's note here that the trips offer different narratives in each direction. When riding from Hogsmeade to London, look out the "window" in your eight-passenger train compartment to see the Weasley twins and Buckbeak flying by, and then watch the Knight Bus careen through the streets of London as your approach King's Cross station in Universal Studios Florida.

## The Three Broomsticks

*Theme Park Insider readers' rating:* 8/10 (Commendable)

Hogsmeade's restaurant recreates a favorite destination for Hogwarts students on their weekend visits to the village. Or, perhaps we might more accurately describe it the other way around: The Three Broomsticks restaurant you saw in the Harry Potter films is a recreation of this restaurant from Islands of Adventure.

That's because Harry Potter film production designer Stuart Craig designed The Three Broomsticks interior set for the movies at the same time that he was working with Universal Creative on the design for the Orlando version. That cooperation allows Universal Orlando visitors to enjoy eating in a restaurant that looks every bit like the one in the films. Of course, a working restaurant must function very differently than a movie set, which lacks four walls, a ceiling, and certainly doesn't include a functioning kitchen. So there is literally more here than meets the eye of a movie-goer.

What about the food, then? The Three Broomsticks is a counter-service restaurant serving traditional British pub fare, including fish and chips, shepherd's pie, and Cornish pasties, as well as smoked chicken, turkey legs, and ribs, from $8-15. There's a "Great Feast" of salad, smoked chicken and ribs, corn on the cob, roasted potatoes, that serves four for about $50. Breakfast (around $15 for adults) is served in the morning and offers Full English and American breakfasts, as well as options for pancakes or porridge.

You will queue in single file, then be directed to one of the registers to place your order. Then you'll pick up your food at a nearby counter before finding a table. (At busy times of the year, a Universal team member will direct you to an open table.)

If there's a single signature food item in the Wizarding World, it is **Butterbeer**. A nonalcoholic concoction, created by Universal Orlando head chef Steve Jayson with the approval of J.K. Rowling, Butterbeer comes in two forms: a cold "regular" style and a slush-like "frozen" version. (If you happen to be visiting during the winter holidays, you might also be offered a warm version, as well.) Either way, Butterbeer is a sweet soft drink that tastes of butterscotch, with maybe a hint of shortbread. It's served with a creamy "head," though there's no dairy in the recipe, according to Universal Orlando spokespersons. There also is no high fructose corn syrup [HFCS] in butterbeer. Unlike most soft drinks served in the United States, the sweetener in Butterbeer is actual cane sugar. J.K. Rowling reportedly demanded that Universal not use HFCS in any Wizarding World food product, which provides one of the reasons why you cannot buy Coca-Cola products in The Three Broomsticks or anywhere else in the Wizarding World lands, despite Coke being the official soft drink of the Universal Orlando Resort.

There's a huge butterbeer cart located outside the front door of The Three Broomsticks, often with a huge line to match. But you can order a butterbeer with your meal (or just by itself) inside The Three Broomsticks, so skip the queue for the cart if the line for the restaurant seems shorter.

Another option is to order your butterbeer at the **Hog's Head Pub**, located adjacent to The Three Broomsticks. The bar also serves pumpkin juice, several ciders, and both Wizard-themed and Muggle beers and cocktails. During very busy seasons, such as the week between Christmas and New Year's, you might be asked to queue for the Hog's Head via the porch behind The Three Broomsticks, rather than entering from the Hogsmeade high street. The back porch is a lovely getaway within the Wizarding World, offering a nice view of the Hogwarts Castle, overlooking the park's central lagoon. If you can't find a place to sit inside the restaurant, don't forget to try the back porch.

Trying to decide what to order? At the official opening of The Wizarding World, Michael Gambon told reporters that his favorite item was the shepherd's pie, while Rupert Grint praised the Treacle Fudge, and Tom Felton endorsed the British-style bacon in the English breakfast. Daniel Radcliffe said that he most preferred the frozen Butterbeer: "And you need it in this unbelievable heat," Harry Potter himself said. "It's very refreshing."

## Ollivander's

Every wizard (or wizard-loving Muggle) needs a magic wand, and the place to buy yours is Ollivander's, "maker of fine wands since 382 B.C." When Hogsmeade opened in 2010, Diagon Alley wasn't even a rumor yet, so Universal concocted a backstory that Ollivander's had opened a satellite location in Hogsmeade to serve the students at Hogwarts. (You might remember that Harry bought his wand from Ollivander's during his initial visit to Diagon Alley in *Harry Potter and the Sorcerer's(Philosopher's) Stone.*)

Hogsmeade's version of Ollivander's, like the much larger version now found in the new Diagon Alley land, offers both a wand shop where you can choose from a selection of wands (including replications of those used by Harry Potter characters), as well as a short show where you can see "a wand choose the wizard," just as happened for Harry on that day, long ago, in 1991. (You did know that Harry Potter was born on July 31, 1980, right? And that Harry shares his birthday with a certain Scottish author?) A young visitor is chosen to be the "wizard" or "witch" that the wand chooses in each show, but with a limited capacity of just about a dozen or so people for each short presentation, the wait for the show became one of the longest in the entire park.

The Diagon Alley version of Ollivander's includes several more rooms, allowing multiple shows to take place at the same time and all but eliminating the wait to watch. The Diagon Alley shop also offers a larger store area, not to mention a Wands by Gregorovitch shop around the corner, for our Slytherin friends. But if you can't wait to buy a wand, and you are starting your visit in Hogsmeade, this version of Ollivander's is still here, and with a fraction of the wait times that it offered before Diagon Alley opened.

You've also got a new choice in wands, since the opening of Diagon Alley. You can buy "traditional" wands for about $35 (the price in late 2014), or you can get one of the new **interactive wands** for $10 more. If you walk around Hogsmeade and Diagon Alley, you might notice small, round brass plates embedded in the ground in front of several store windows around the lands. If you've got one of the interactive wands, you can stand just behind the plate and cast the spell described on the plate with your wand to trigger a "magical" animation effect in the window. There are 34 such locations throughout the two lands, and you'll get a map to them, which includes some instructions, when you buy an interactive wand.

## Other Shops in Hogsmeade Village

**Filch's Emporium of Confiscated Goods** is the gift shop at the exit of "Harry Potter and the Forbidden Journey," though you don't need to ride to browse the store's selection of Hogwarts House T-shirts and other Hogwarts-logo clothing, Quidditch shirts, Wizard chess sets, prop replicas, Hogwarts stationery and gifts, and magical creature toys. Just walk past the ride entrance, toward the entrance to the "Flying Hippogriff." You'll find the entrance to Filch's to the left.

**Dervish and Banges** offers magical toys, including Sneakoscopes and Spectrespecs; Quidditch supplies, including brooms, Quaffles, Golden Snitches, and shirts, plus Hogwarts school uniforms, as well as other wizard-themed stationery, toys, and gifts. You'll find Dervish and Banges next to Ollivander's, across the High Street from The Three Broomsticks.

**Honeydukes** is your stop for sweets in The Wizarding World. Located next to The Three Broomsticks, Universal expanded this shop in the spring of 2014, having it take over the adjacent space previously occupied by the now-gone Zonko's Joke Shop. (Weasleys' Wizard Wheezes in Diagon Alley now serves your wizarding joke shop needs.) Popular items at Honeydukes include Chocolate Frogs (with a wizard trading card in every box!), Bertie Bott's Every-Flavour Beans, Acid Pops, Ton Tongue Toffee, Peppermint Frogs, Candy Floss, Chocolate Wands, and a selection of other candies. (You can grab a bag and fill it with your choice of the hard and gummy candies and licorice.) Cold, bottled Pumpkin Juice is available, and inside the service case you'll find Chocolate Cauldrons, Rocks Cakes, Treacle Fudge, and Candied Apples.

*A dragon stands guard atop Gringotts Bank in The Wizarding World of Harry Potter — Diagon Alley at Universal Studios Florida*

# THE WIZARDING WORLD OF HARRY POTTER — DIAGON ALLEY

With the amazing success of Hogsmeade, Universal moved quickly to expand the Harry Potter franchise to other theme parks. In December 2011, Universal announced that the Wizarding World would come to Universal Studios Hollywood in Los Angeles. And that same month, rumors began to fly that Universal would close the Jaws ride at Universal Studios Florida, to replace it with another Harry Potter land.

On December 31, 2011, ThemeParkInsider.com first published plans leaked to us of a second Wizarding World of Harry Potter, to be themed to London's Diagon Alley. Located on the site of the soon-to-be closed Jaws ride in Universal Studios Florida, this second Harry Potter land would be connected to the original Hogsmeade-themed Wizarding World via a Hogwarts Express train that would run between the two theme parks. Filled with even more shops that in Hogsmeade, Diagon Alley also would include Gringotts Bank, which would be the home to a new ride, featuring a hybrid of roller coaster and motion base ride systems, coupled with 3D filmed scenes and practical effects. Universal confirmed the construction of the new land in May 2013. The Wizarding World of Harry Potter — Diagon Alley opened officially to the public on July 8, 2014, following a media preview on June 18-19, 2014.

Keeping true to its source material, Diagon Alley is hidden from the rest of the "Muggle" world in Universal Studios Florida. It stands behind a stunning facade of famous London buildings, including King's Cross station and the Wyndham's Theater. You might recognize Grimmauld Place off to the right, too. Take a moment to stare into the windows of Number 12 Grimmauld Place. You might see Kreacher the house elf peeking through the curtains. The only other hint of something magical nearby? The purple Knight Bus, parked in front of the theater, where you might be able to meet Stan Shunpike, or chat up the shrunken heads behind the windshield.

Take note of the Leicester Square Tube station, too, for behind that, next to the faded sign for The Leaky Cauldron, lies your portal into The Wizarding World.

The Wizarding World of Harry Potter — Diagon Alley resets the standard for theme park environments, creating a wildly engaging setting that rewards visitors willing to delve into the abundant detail to be found in the new land. No other theme park land in the world offers the level of detail Universal Orlando has packed into this new Harry Potter-themed land. Not even the original Wizarding World over at Islands of Adventure comes close to Diagon Alley in creating such an authentically convincing experience. As actress Evanna Lynch [Luna Lovegood] noted during the press event, "you don't see roller coaster tracks" in this Harry Potter land. It's a faithful creation of what J.K. Rowling described in her Harry Potter books and creative artists Stuart Craig and Alan Gilmore designed for the Potter films.

Most theme parks find ways to "suggest to express," using tricks such as forced perspectives to make locations seem grander than they are. But there are few such shortcuts here. The ceiling of The Leaky Cauldron restaurant, for example, soars above its customers, a full two stories above your head. And you certainly won't be able to overlook the life-sized, fire-breathing Ukrainian Ironbelly dragon perched atop Gringotts Bank, creating one of the great photo-ops in the theme park industry.

In the Harry Potter books and movies, Diagon Alley was the Wizarding World's mall, and there is much for sale here, including $45 interactive wands that trigger animation effects in selected windows here and in Hogsmeade. But don't dismiss this Diagon Alley as just a place to buy Potter-themed souvenirs. Whether it's cars, cosplay, or theme park souvenirs, many of us love to express our passions through purchases. We buy this stuff because we want to *feel* authentic, and all this stuff around us helps to feel that. Harry Potter fans want their wands, their robes, their house scarves, and their Butterbeers. Universal (or some other theme park company) could have slapped some posters on a wall, piled stock-ordered desks with merchandise, ordered an off-the-shelf ride system with a Harry Potter skin, and raked in the cash.

But Universal didn't do that. Instead of letting us into Harry Potter's world to meet *its* needs of selling stuff, Universal sells stuff because it met *our* need to get into Harry Potter's world. Ask the thousands of cosplaying fans who lined up for hours to get into Hogsmeade and Diagon Alley when they opened for the first time. Ask the actors who stand slack-jawed on a Diagon Alley street, awed by the complete physical realization of what their films had tried to portray. There's a magic here, of being in a place that transports your imagination into something it even more easily accepts as reality.

To call this a theme park land diminishes it, for Diagon Alley exceeds anything ever before carrying that label. To fans longing to become part of the stories of their dreams, this *is* the Wizarding World of Harry Potter.

## Hogwarts Express: London to Hogsmeade

*Theme Park Insider readers' rating:* 9/10 (Outstanding)
*No minimum height to ride*

As Universal Orlando's new Wizarding World of Harry Potter — Diagon Alley breaks new ground for theme park lands, the accompanying Hogwarts Express might best be considered as breaking walls within the theme park industry. While many have written about the Hogwarts Express as part of the Diagon Alley project, it's really not part of the Diagon Alley land within the park. Universal's Hogwarts Express connects the two Wizarding Worlds via stations *adjacent* to those lands, in Islands of Adventure and Universal Studios Florida. It leaves from Universal Studios Florida via the King's Cross station located adjacent to Diagon Alley.

And it's inside that King's Cross station where the Hogwarts Express station breaks its first wall — the wall between the Wizarding and "Muggle" (non-magical) worlds. King's Cross stands firmly in the Muggle world, and Universal has faithfully recreated a London train station, complete with uniformed attendants, directional signs and brickwork straight from the original King's Cross station in London.

The Universal team members at the King's Cross entrance play their roles convincingly, commenting with bewilderment at visitors' "strange sticks" and "funny robes." As Muggles, they know nothing of the Wizarding World, so of course they shouldn't recognize magic wands and house robes when the see witches and wizards with them. Yet the ride attendants will send visitors down the tunnel toward platforms nine and 10, figuring that these strange people will just need to see for themselves that there is no "Platform 9 3/4."

Once you get upstairs, you will find that Universal has crafted a nifty effect to allow visitors to pass through that wall that separates the Muggle and Wizard worlds. It's a Pepper's Ghost-style mirror effect that allows people in the queue to see those ahead seemingly pass through a solid brick wall to that Platform 9 3/4. And here, Universal breaks another wall with the Hogwarts Express — that "wall" that separates audience from performer.

Universal long ago claimed audience participation in its shows as part of its identity. But it's one thing to pick someone from the audience to play "Mother" in *Psycho* or an extra in a fake Rice-A-Roni commercial (to cite two roles I've played over the years in Universal attractions as an audience volunteer); it's much more ambitious to cast everyone in the queue as individual players in a practical special effect. Yet each person walking through the queue gets his or her chance to walk through that wall. (While those behind will see you disappear through the wall, you'll simply walk through a zig-zag in the queue, as a whooshing sound plays over the speakers in the ceiling and the mirrors do their work with your reflection.)

Once around that corner, you're on Platform 9 3/4 from the Harry Potter films, with wizards and witches wearing Hogwarts Express conductor costumes, instead of the British Rail costumes on the "Muggle" attendants you encountered before.

You'll soon board the train to take your seat in the eight-passenger compartments that look just like those Harry, Ron, and Hermione occupied in *Harry Potter and the Sorcerer's (or Philosopher's) Stone*. The Express train is, inside and out, a faithful visual recreation of the Jacobite locomotive and coaches featured in the Harry Potter films. Now it's time for you to journey, as they did, from Muggle London to the wizarding village of Hogsmeade and the Hogwarts School of Witchcraft and Wizardry.

The effect of watching the English and Scottish countrysides pass is utterly convincing, with physical space between the train windows and the passing scenes. While seats in the middle of the train compartments offer the ideal views, there's enough parallax effect that the scenery convinces from every seat. And don't neglect to turn around when you hear voices in the corridor. You'll find the shadows of familiar characters walking down the corridors as you ride.

The Hogwarts Express offers distinct journeys in each direction. On the trip from London to Hogsmeade, you'll encounter Dementors, watch Chocolate Frogs escape from the sweets cart, and see Hagrid flying on

Sirius Black's motorbike just outside your window, on his way to greet you at Hogsmeade Station.

And now Universal breaks yet another wall — a conceptual one that traditionally has defined theme parks as distinct destinations. It's become convention for theme park attractions to drop you off at or very near the same point where you boarded the ride, so it's a bit disorienting when you exit the Hogwarts Express and find that you're not only in a different train station — you're in a different theme park.

Some fans have complained about Universal requiring visitors to have bought a park-to-park ticket to ride the Hogwarts Express. They've grown accustomed to saving money by declining "park-to-park" or "park-hopper" options and enjoying one park per day. But Universal is breaking the walls that separate theme parks, to reinvent its Orlando resort as single destination where its two theme parks are joined as one by the Wizarding World of Harry Potter that spans both. Yes, that forces a different pricing structure, but it opens new creative possibilities in return.

Yes, the one-day price for Universal Orlando's park-to-park tickets is steep — $136 for visitors age 10 and older, as of this book's publication. Unless you're staying at a Universal Orlando hotel where you get unlimited Universal Express front-of-line access, there's no way to see all that the resort's parks have to offer in a single day, making such a purchase a poor value. And even with unlimited Express access, one day would offer only a hectic rush of merely the highlights, anyway. The far better buys are the two- and three-day park-to-park tickets (at $176 and $186, respectively), which allow you to treat these two parks within walking distance as one, with enough time and flexibility to enjoy both.

If you want the full experience of The Wizarding World of Harry Potter, you're going to have to experience it on Universal's terms, and that means a park-to-park ticket, and probably spending more than one day at the parks. But Universal is delivering extraordinary value in return for that purchase, giving you the best themed land in the world as well as a captivating new ride in the Hogwarts Express that presents a dens... transit between Universal Studios Florida's London and Islands of Adventure's Scottish highlands.

## Harry Potter and the Escape from Gringotts

*Theme Park Insider readers' rating:* 9/10 (Outstanding)
*Minimum height to ride: 42 inches*

Author Tom Stoppard built his popular reputation with *Rosencrantz and Guildenstern Are Dead*, a retelling of Shakespeare's *Hamlet* from the perspective of two minor characters in that enduring tragedy. That can be a clever device, allowing us to see a familiar story from a fresh angle. But what if that fresh perspective were not that of a minor character from the famous story, but that of the reader him- or herself?

That's the set-up for "Harry Potter and the Escape from Gringotts," a new thrill ride in Universal Studios Florida's Wizarding World of Harry Potter — Diagon Alley. Universal Creative has crafted much more than a thrill ride here — it's retold a classic tale from your perspective.

The familiar story is from *Harry Potter and the Deathly Hallows*, where Harry, Ron, and Hermione con their way into Gringotts Bank to steal (and, ultimately, destroy) the Horcrux in Bellatrix Lestrange's vault, the enchanted Hufflepuff Cup that holds one-eighth of evil Lord Voldemort's soul.

By a coincidence unknown until the opening of Universal Studios Florida's new land, that also happens to be the same day that we, fellow Diagon Alley visitors, have chosen to visit Gringotts to open our own accounts. Like in Stoppard's creation, we have a minor character on board with us here, too, as we've got an appointment with Ron's little-seen older brother Bill Weasley to tour the bank's underground vaults. Actor Domhnall Gleeson reprised his role for several filmed scenes in the ride and queue, including his initial sales pitch to us for Gringotts, "it's the safest place on Earth!"

What *possibly* could go wrong?

Our visit begins innocuously enough, with a stroll through Gringotts' opulent Great Hall, where animatronic goblins sit perched above eye level, hard at work, while we gawk at the stunning detail in their faces and movements. From the Great Hall, we proceed down to the bank's offices, where attendants take our photos for our bank record (and, yes, for the end-of-ride souvenir sale), before we head down the hall to Bill's office.

The preshow scene will be familiar to anyone who has visited Dumbledore's office in "Harry Potter and the Forbidden Journey" at Universal's Islands of Adventure. Practical sets in front of a screen create a three-dimensional feel as we watch Bill welcome us to Gringotts and set up our tour of the vaults below.

From Weasley's office, it's into one of a pair of lifts (a.k.a. elevators, for the Americans) for the trip 10 miles down into the Gringotts vaults. It's an appropriately hammy trip, with shaking floors and video effects creating the illusion of a reckless plummet. When the doors open, we walk up a spiral staircase to the loading platform, where we board one of the twin, 12-person roller coaster trains for our tour.

Then, of course, it all goes terribly wrong.

Our heroes have been detected, and Gringotts' security defenses are coming to life. Bellatrix herself appears as we're about to launch into the ride, to curse us as potential accomplices to the theft of her vault.

Fortunately, our new friend Bill is near, to save us from hurtling into oblivion with an "arresto momentum." Escape from Gringotts plays on a creative ride system that incorporates a roller coaster track with embedded motion bases in several spots, allowing a unique range of motion that leads you to forget about the ride itself and focus instead on your role in the attraction's grand story. The action takes place on 3D screens, set amid richly detailed practical sets of the Gringotts caverns.

Our rescue lasts but a moment before the Gringotts trolls attack, mistaking us for the intruders. We're thrown through The Thief's Downfall, before another troll attack sends us plunging hundreds of feet toward our certain doom upon the rock-strewn rapids that churn upon the floor of the caverns.

We're not really falling, though. It's just the combination of the motion-base vehicle and the 3D animation at work, as on Universal's "The Amazing Adventures of Spider-Man" and "Transformers: The Ride 3D." But the setting and 3D technology work even more convincingly here, making the moment of our rescue (again!) all the more thrilling.

Bill sends us off to a vault for safety, and it's at that moment that Escape from Gringotts takes us to another level of emotional engagement. The hissing of the snake Nagini warns us of the arrival of Bellatrix and He-Who-Must-Not-Be-Named, Lord Voldemort.

Helena Bonham Carter and Ralph Fiennes work among the "A" team of Harry Potter actors, two superb professionals who have crafted utterly captivating villains, and Universal has brought them on board to reprise their roles for this ride. To see these two at work in these characters again would by itself be a joy. But larger than life and in sharp three-dimensional projection? I could watch them here all day.

If they weren't trying to kill us, of course.

Bellatrix curses us away, though we soon discover that the pair are only toying with us. As we lurch into the next cavern, the evil duo arrives again, riding plumes of black smoke, to torture us to a fiery death. We are spared only when Harry, Ron and Hermione — atop their recently-hijacked dragon — find us, directing the dragon to fend off Voldemort's fireball. Hermione throws us a chain, and the dragon hauls us up out of the cavern to safety. It's a thrilling final launch through the wall of the cavern into our final scene. There, Bill greets us with congratulations and a final, now ironic, repeat of his sales pitch to open an account: "It's the safest place on Earth!"

Yeah, right. But if Gringotts really were that safe, it wouldn't be nearly as much fun.

## Carkitt Market Stage

*Theme Park Insider readers' rating:* 9/10 (Outstanding)

While Universal's Hogsmeade Village has only one main street, you will find four main "streets" in Diagon Alley: Diagon Alley itself, which extends from the land's entrance to Gringotts Bank; Horizont Alley, which intersects Diagon Alley in front of Gringotts; the ever-darkened Knockturn Alley, which you'll discover after turning left onto Horizont Alley; and Carkitt Market, a covered marketplace at the end of Horizont Alley on the right, as you face Gringotts Bank.

There's a small stage at the side of Carkitt Market, which hosts a pair of shows throughout the day. **Celestina Warbeck and the Banshees**, name-checked in *Harry Potter and the Half-Blood Prince* for hits such as "A Cauldron Full of Hot, Strong Love," perform in concert in one show. (J.K. Rowling has said that the character of Celestina was inspired by Welsh singer Shirley Bassey, perhaps best known for singing the theme song to the James Bond film *Goldfinger.*) The other on the Carkitt Market stage is a performance of **Tales from Beedle the Bard**, including a stunning puppet performance of "Tale of the Three Brothers," from *Harry Potter and the Deathly Hallows*. Check Universal's show schedule (available at the front entrance turnstiles or any store register in the park) for showtimes.

## The Leaky Cauldron

*Theme Park Insider readers' rating:* 9/10 (Outstanding)

A recreation of the London pub that served as the gateway to Diagon Alley, The Leaky Cauldron is a counter-service restaurant serving a variety of British pub fare, as well as many Wizard-themed speciality drinks.

Too often in theme parks, the theme extends only to a restaurant's decor, while the menu sells out to presumed consumer favorites, including the ubiquitous burgers, hot dogs, and pizza that populate most theme park menus. The original Wizarding World challenged that convention, even going so far as to banish products from Universal's soft-drink partner, Coca-Cola. You won't find chicken nuggets and hot dogs on menus in the Wizarding World, either in Hogsmeade or Diagon Alley. The Leaky Cauldon's menu instead offers choices such as:

- Bangers and Mash [sausages and mashed potatoes]
- Toad in the Hole [sausage in savory pastry]
- Cottage Pie [beef and vegetables under a mashed-potato topping]
- Fisherman's Pie [same thing, but with seafood instead]
- Beef, Lamb & Guinness Stew [served in a bread bowl]
- Ploughman's Lunch [a selection of cheeses, pickles, bread, and a Scotch egg — a hard-boiled egg wrapped in a thin layer of sausage and deep fried]
- Split Pea Soup
- Fish and Chips

Desserts include Chocolate Potted Cream and Sticky Toffee Pudding. Breakfast also is served in the morning, including Apple Oatmeal Flan with Yogurt and Fruit, and an Egg, Leek and Mushroom Pasty.

Yes, you'll find Butterbeer here, but you'll also find new concoctions, too, such as Fishy Green Ale, a minty bubble tea beverage with "fish eggs" (blueberry-flavored bubbles) at the bottom. The alcoholic options include Wizard's Brew (a stout) and Dragon Scale (a Vienna lager) —

both from Florida Beer Company, which also makes the Duff Beer in Universal Studios Florida's Simpsons-themed Springfield USA land. If you're wondering which of the many strangely-named speciality drinks include alcohol and which do not, here's a simple and effective tip: look at the price. If the price of a drink (not including a souvenir cup) is under five bucks, there's no booze in it. Hey, you get what you pay for.

If you are ordering a meal, in good British pub style you will place your order at the bar. Then, for the wizarding twist, you will be given a numbered candlestick to take to a table, where a team member will bring your food when it is ready.

## Other Places to Eat and Drink in Diagon Alley

When Harry Potter stayed at The Leaky Cauldron for several weeks before the start of school in *Harry Potter and the Prisoner of Azkaban*, he often walked down Diagon Alley to **Florean Fortescue's Ice-Cream Parlour** for a frozen snack. You can choose from a selection of unique flavors (including Butterbeer ice cream) at this shop, located across the way from Gringotts Bank. Other flavors include Earl Grey Lavender and Chocolate Chili. Next door to Fortescue's, on Horizont Alley, is **The Fountain of Fair Fortune**, a small indoor pub that serves Butterbeer and Butterbeer ice cream, plus a selection of beers and cocktails.

As Horizont Alley transitions into Carkitt Market, in the other direction, you will find **Eternelle's Elixir of Refreshment**, a small stand serving Gilly Water. Gilly Water is just plain bottled water, but for about an extra $4, you can buy a flavored elixir to "transform" your drink. (Ask for the keepsake vial, if your server pours in the elixir himself and neglects to offer it to you.) The elixir options include:

- Babbling Beverage (red) - tropical fruit punch
- Draught of Peace (blue) - mixed berry with a bit of cherry
- Elixir to Induce Euphoria (green) - pineapple with green apple and mint

- Fire Protection Potion (orange) - watermelon with peach and strawberry

At the end of Carkitt Market, you'll find one more option for drinks, **The Hopping Pot**, which serves The Leaky Cauldron's drink menu.

## Ollivander's

An expanded version of the wand shop in Hogsmeade. In Harry Potter canon, this is the "original" version of Ollivander's, even though in reality, the Hogsmeade store opened four years before this one in Diagon Alley. No matter, Potter canon tells us that Ollivander's has been selling fine wands *somewhere* since 382 B.C., and we're just going to buy in and believe that.

You can participate in the same "wand chooses the wizard" show here as in Hogsmeade, or chose from a selection of character wands, or buy one of the new interactive wands that allow you to trigger animation effects in windows around the land. Ask for a demonstration of the interactive wands, and maybe a short lesson, too, as wizards and witches in training sometime find it a bit tricky to get the hang of swishing-and-flicking their wands properly.

## Gringotts Money Exchange

Money, of course, plays a prominent role in Diagon Alley. (Its centerpiece is a bank, after all.) Around the corner from Gringotts Bank, in Carkitt Market, you'll find the Gringotts Money Exchange, where a goblin animatronic behind the counter interacts with guests, answering their questions about this money exchange. Yes, you really can swap your Muggle $10s and $20s for equivalent Gringotts Bank Notes, accepted at stores throughout the Wizarding World (and elsewhere in the Universal Orlando Resort, for that matter.)

It's a gimmick Disney tried first more than two decades ago with its

Disney Dollars. But it makes far more sense here, as a more authentic element to draw you into the role of a visitor to Diagon Alley. Think of it as cosplay for your wallet.

## Other Shops in Diagon Alley

With the closing of Zonko's in Hogsmeade, your home for wizarding tricks and novelties in the Wizarding World is **Weasleys' Wizard Wheezes**, located to your right as you enter Diagon Alley. Topped with the same grinning wizard, ever doffing his hat, as we first saw in *Harry Potter and the Half-Blood Prince*, Weasley's offers magical toys and gags from the books and films, including U-No-Poo, Skiving Snackboxes, and Pygmy Puffs.

Of course, if you've been sorted into Slytherin, you'd rather serve 100 detentions with Minerva McGonagall than visit the Weasley's shop. So turn instead down Knockturn Alley to visit **Borgin and Burkes**, the home of dark magic in Diagon Alley. Decorated with prop and costume replicas from the films, including Death Eater masks and robes, Borgin and Burkes sells apparel, jewelry, gifts, and collectibles for any dark magic-loving fan.

If you'd prefer not attracting the attention of Ministry of Magic aurors when walking through Diagon Alley, consider instead outfitting yourself at **Madam Malkin's Robes for All Occasions**, located between The Leaky Cauldron and Florean Fortescue's. The is the place to buy your Hogwarts house robes, scarves, sweaters, and other house-themed apparel. Madam Malkin also offers a wild selection of hats for the fashionable wizard or witch.

Up the street, across from Florean Fortescue's on Horizont Alley, is **Magical Menagerie**, selling plush versions of many favorite magical pets, including owls, cats, and even rats. You can buy toy versions of Cornish pixies, Fang, and Buckbeak, too. Take a few moments, also, to watch the many animatronic animals in the windows and on the walls throughout the shop.

**Wiseacre's Wizarding Equipment** is the shop at the exit of "Harry Potter and the Escape from Gringotts." Highlighted by a wonderful collection of wizarding astronomy equipment on its ceiling, Wiseacre's sells telescopes, crystal balls, hourglasses, and other magical equipment and gifts.

Need a new Bludger bat? A Quaffle? You'll find those, along with a variety of brooms and Quidditch sweaters from many favorite teams, at **Quality Quidditch Supplies**, located next to Weasley's.

Not happy with the selection at Ollivander's? Looking for something a bit, well, darker? You'll find the small **Wands by Gregorovitch** walk-up store located in Carkitt Market, around the corner from Weasley's.

Aspiring writers and thoughtful Hogwarts students can find quills, stationery and other writing supplies at **Scribbulus**, located next to Wiseacre's.

Finally, you can star in your own Harry Potter DVD by dressing up and posing in front of the green screen in **Shutterbutton's**, located in Carkitt Market, behind Weasley's and Quality Quidditch.

*Thierry Coup, center, of Universal Creative talks about The Wizarding World as Mark Woodbury, left, and Alan Gilmore look on.*

# DESIGNERS AND ACTORS TALK ABOUT THE WIZARDING WORLD

Let's hear now from some of the creative team that designed and built The Wizarding World. Universal Creative, which is the division of Universal Studios that designs and develops its theme parks and attractions, led the project, with assistance from some of the production team from the Harry Potter films. At the opening of each Wizarding World land, Universal Orlando held a series of press conferences with selected reporters invited to talk with the creators behind these new lands. In addition, Universal hosted several of the stars of the Harry Potter movies, who also met with the press to talk about the lands. We were there at all of those press events, and include selected comments from them in this chapter. In addition, we've included comments from one-on-one interviews and conversations we've had with Universal Creative leaders, as well as theme park design professionals from other companies.

Here is a list of people we will hear from in this chapter. From Universal Creative:

- **Mark Woodbury**, *President*
- **Thierry Coup**, *Senior Vice President*
- **Dale Mason**, *Vice President Creative Executive Art Director*

From the Harry Potter film production team:

- **David Barron**, *Producer*
- **David Heyman**, *Producer*
- **Stuart Craig**, *Production Designer*
- **Alan Gilmore**, *Supervising Art Director*

Stars of the Harry Potter films:

- **Helena Bonham Carter**, *Bellatrix Lestrange*
- **Robbie Coltrane**, *Rubeus Hagrid*
- **Tom Felton**, *Draco Malfoy*
- **Michael Gambon**, *Albus Dumbledore*
- **Domhnall Gleeson**, *Bill Weasley*
- **Matthew Lewis**, *Neville Longbottom*
- **Evanna Lynch**, *Luna Lovegood*
- **James Phelps**, *Fred Weasley*
- **Daniel Radcliffe**, *Harry Potter*
- **Bonnie Wright**, *Ginny Weasley*

From outside Universal:

- **Tony Baxter**, *Former Senior Vice President of Walt Disney Imagineering.* Baxter was the lead designer of many classic Disney attractions, including "Big Thunder Mountain Railroad," "Star Tours," and "Splash Mountain." While he was at Disney, the company's Imagineers developed their own plans for a Harry Potter-themed attraction at the Walt Disney World Resort, before Universal won the rights.
- **Dave Cobb**, *Senior Creative Director at Thinkwell Group.* Thinkwell Group produced the "Making of Harry Potter" tour at Warner Bros.' Leavesden Studios in the United Kingdom, as well as the opening-ceremony shows for Hogsmeade and Diagon Alley in Orlando. Before joining Thinkwell, Cobb worked for Universal

Creative, where he was the lead designer for "Men in Black Alien Attack," located near Diagon Alley in Universal Studios Florida.

And now, The Wizarding World, in the words of those most connected to the projects:

**Mark Woodbury**, *President of Universal Creative* — From the onset, J.K. Rowling was a critical part of the process and remained that way throughout everything we did. And she really had great participation in the process from beginning to end.

**David Heyman**, *Producer of the Harry Potter films* — One of the great things about Jo is that she understands that films are different than the books, and she understands that a theme park is different than the books. She is the most generous of collaborators, really encouraging Universal and the entire team to do what they can, everything they can, within the opportunities that present themselves within a theme park.

**Woodbury** — Before Potter was a seven-book, eight-film franchise, we already knew that it was going to be a great theme park. That was after just the first book. On one hand, you'd like to know that you have a proven franchise, with tremendous box office results, but in the case of Potter that really wasn't it. We knew it had the makings of a great theme park experience because of the characters, because of the action, because of the magical places that Jo Rowling created.

**Stuart Craig**, *Production Designer for the Harry Potter films* — Ten years ago, she gave you (addressing David Heyman) and I a map. We met her for the first time and had stacks of questions and she drew a map of the [wizarding] world, which I still have and I'm sure you have your copy. [Laughing with Heyman] That really did lay out the relationship of Hogsmeade Village, Hogwarts Castle, the winged boars, the gateway, where the train station is, how the first years go across by water and enter the school by water, and everyone else goes round in carriages — the whole thing that all the devotees of the books now understand. She set that in this very clear map.

**Heyman** — It's really useful for us. It's fantastic. When we were doing the fifth film, the Black family tree, we'd go to Jo and say, 'In the book there are three or four names, can you help us?' Because in the film we were going to show more. Fifteen minutes later this family tree with 100 names — birthdays, death days, who's married to whom — arrived on my computer. Her knowledge of this world is so rich. One of things I love about this theme park is the detail. Everywhere you look there's a little bit that comes from Jo Rowling, because her books are so detailed and so rich. And the way that Thierry [Coup, of Universal Creative] and his team, and Mark, have built on it is fantastic.

**Tom Felton**, *Draco Malfoy* — [The Wizarding World] was a rumor for a long time, I didn't know if it was true. Then Thierry came down (to the set) at the end of six [*Harry Potter and the Half-Blood Prince*], and then it was on.

**Daniel Radcliffe**, *Harry Potter* — We had a big meeting where we talked through the plans for the park. My reaction when we heard that this was going to be a thing was, "Well, that's, okay." You don't know what that's going to entail, how that's going to end up. When we were filming it [the scenes for Forbidden Journey], we were very much aware of the depth, the attention to detail — and the care that was taken over the building of this place is equal to what we do for the films. That's what's been very gratifying to come here and see. Being so involved in it, it is really nice to see that it is in such safe hands. It's very much authentic, and wonderful.

[For Forbidden Journey,] we did about a month or so of extra filming at the end of Harry Potter 6, which was known brilliantly as the "Strong Arm Unit." [That's a reference to the Kuka robot arms that carry each ride vehicle.] It was very weird because it was treated in a way that we're not used to — we were told to talk into the camera and stuff you're generally encouraged not to do. And yeah, it was a kind of new experience. The technology they are using in this is quite amazing, I mean we are kind of physically there, particularly in Dumbledore's office. And I always have to point out the irony of having Michael Gambon do any safety instructions or information. [Laughter]

**Michael Gambon**, *Albus Dumbledore* — I don't abide by them myself. [More laughter] I just say what they tell me to say. [Grins]

**Matthew Lewis**, *Neville Longbottom* — To be in a film is one thing, and I guess that will last forever and ever, but to be on a ride, it's something else. I've loved coming to theme parks, roller coasters and stuff like that since I was tiny. So to be a part of something like that that's going to be halfway around the world in America, I'm still trying to figure that out in my head, it's kind of weird. But it's unbelievable, to be there in something that will last for decades yet. A great privilege.

**James Phelps**, *Fred Weasley* — It was probably round about two years ago that we shot the film that's in here, in Forbidden Journey. The guys were showing us the plans for the ride and we saw all the information and thought, surely this is too good to be true. My favorite ride ever was the Spider-Man ride here, and they said it would be like that, but 10 years' technology on top of that. So we thought we would take that with a pinch of salt, and then when we went on Forbidden Journey, that blew us away completely. We've got a good little checklist of what we're in now: We're in a movie, we're in a theme park, we're Lego men... [Laughter]

**Woodbury** — In Forbidden Journey, we wanted to capture the most dynamic parts of the fiction. What makes for a great attraction is the same thing that makes for great movies — you have wonderful characters, these magical places, and really spellbinding action. So for us to be able to take all that and weave it together into a ride experience involved picking iconographic moments from the fiction and weaving it into a story that would allow us to exaggerate those and to make them everything we wanted them to be in terms of a takeaway experience. Flying was critical. Going into the Forbidden Forest was great. Coming face to face with Dementors was something. We knew everybody would want to be in the middle of a Quidditch match. And to do all that while you were able to become up-close and personal to the characters was everything about making a great ride.

**Radcliffe** — There's a moment [on Forbidden Journey] — I think it's fantastically clever — where the Dementors come to take out your soul and you see your own face dragged out in front of you.

**Felton** — That's very cool. I don't know how they do that, but it's very, very cool. The whole seamlessness between real and "fake" — it kind of blows your mind a bit.

**Radcliffe** — It was good that it was quite loud, so I don't have to hear myself scream. If I want to, I can tune myself out, which I try to as often as I can. [Grins]

**Woodbury** — Oftentimes you go down a path technologically to tell a story and you get to a point when they're not quite lining up. You might have this really cool visceral experience and you might have this really cool story, but they're not necessarily building on each other. And there comes a moment in time when you have to make some hard decisions.

There was some of that on Forbidden Journey. When we were doing Forbidden Journey, we knew that the technology [Kuka robot arms] we were going to use to tell the story was the right technology, but there's nuance to that, there's subsets to the technological challenge, part of that has to do with dispatching and all that stuff. Because we were using a really small, four-passenger vehicle, we're dispatching very quickly, but we wanted to make sure that we had an individual experience. We didn't want to see a lot of the vehicles going around. At the same time, we wanted to spend a lot of time with the characters.

So we had to find a way — and this was a revelation way later in the process than we would have liked [laughs] — but we came to a point in time where we were not spending enough time with the characters, and we knew how important that was to the experience and to the storytelling. So we abandoned the direction we were going and created a new direction.

We were struggling and struggling with how to solve this problem, and the more we worked on it, the more evident the problem became. Finally, somebody broke through and said, 'What if we do this?' [Mark would not confirm this, but I am inferring that he is talking about the use of separate curved screens that travel with each individual robot arm during certain sections of the ride.] We pretty much dropped everything we were doing and built a mock-up to see if we could pull off the interface of this vehicle and those media moments. And the reason to do that was to get more time on screen, more time with the vehicle and the characters together in order to really bring the story to life and give you the opportunity to fly alongside Harry and Ron and do all that stuff. Figuring out how to create that interface happened way later in the process — it was a totally different ride experience before, and then we hit that, and we were like, 'That's it.'

**Gambon** — I haven't been yet [on Forbidden Journey]. I've been on the roller coaster — the Dragon [Challenge]. It was terrifying. I just locked myself [curls his arms around himself]. I did not look. It was so frightening. As soon as I got on it, I knew I'd made a mistake. [Laughs]

**Woodbury** — In a process this long, it's fascinating to see the moments of brilliance that happen amongst a collaborative team. There are a few that, for me, jump out in particular. The idea of linking the two parks with the train, that was a ground-breaking thought. When we were thinking about how to make Gringotts different from Forbidden Journey and the idea of bringing Bellatrix and Voldemort into that scene, to come face to face with them and to make this a little bit more about that drama — that was a stroke of brilliance. And when Dale and Stuart discussed putting a dragon on top of the Gringotts Bank, and we were all in London to look at the model, we said we *have* to do this, and it *has* to breathe fire. Those are just the highlights of sparks and fireworks that go off in the course of a project like this.

**Dale Mason**, *Vice President Creative Executive at Universal Creative* — I think that the dragon was the easiest 'yes' in this whole project.

**Woodbury** — It was one of the most complex 'yes'-es, but the easiest one to say, 'we have to find out a way to do this.'

**Tony Baxter**, *Former Senior Vice President of Walt Disney Imagineering* — Well, the biggest misstep — well, we've got to be careful how we say this one — I won't say a word, but it looks a lot like this.

[At this point, Tony goes to his desk and picks up a large booklet labeled "Walt Disney Imagineering: Harry Potter Plans," with an illustration of a Hogsmeade-like land on the front. I show the greatest restraint of my professional life in not lunging across the table to grab the plans from his grasp. Instead, I clench every reflex in my body, to allow Tony to continue talking.]

**Baxter** — I think that people have learned from Disney that, in the end, you don't win by going cheap or avoiding what it is that is currently relevant to an audience. We've talked a lot about the young people of probably your age [Generation Xers, born between 1965-1977], who were into *Star Wars* and the Indiana Jones thing. But now there are people who have come of age between 2000 and now for whom the world of Harry Potter was incredibly influential. I talk a lot at UCLA, and when I do — they're very sophisticated kids, with their iPads and whatnot — and I say, 'how many of you stood in line at Barnes and Noble at midnight on release day?' Over half the class! You bought a book, now I'm told that you don't read anymore... so what was it? It was compelling IP [intellectual property] — and the fact that I don't want to be left out when the kids are all discussing tomorrow what Hermione did and all this stuff. I've got to know.

She [J.K. Rowling] was so thorough in creating a believable world, it was just like Disney in the theme parks. Things like Remembralls, and Howlers, and all these things — they were so classic in the way the world was constructed that they stick in your brain. Whereas I look at the world of *Lord of the Rings*, and, other than the Orcs, I can't tell you the names of the people. They were too confusing. But the Potter world — it's the kind of thing you have to look at and say, once in a lifetime a project like that comes [along] and becomes the relevant myth for a generation.

What I saw was that not only did Universal take advantage of that, but it was IP that was owned by Warner Bros. and J.K. Rowling, so they had to go out on a limb to procure it. In the end, what they've done is link that park with one of the major demographics that go to theme parks today. We all have to stand back and take note. So you see Disney throwing depth charges back — with Cars Land and soon *Avatar*, and a new Fantasyland. I think competition is healthy, no matter where it happens, because people get comfortable, and it takes things like that to shake it up. Again, you can't spend enough money on Harry Potter for that generation, because they will go to the Nth degree to relive their childhood. I don't think anyone has done a better job that they did in bringing that to life. And I'm actually very excited to see what [Diagon Alley] looks like.

**Woodbury** — Gringotts was important to us to bring alive, and it carried with us the opportunity to tell a specific story and use that as a chance to make it very different from Forbidden Journey. It was a tricky piece of business to find a way to do that, that would be authentic, so we studied it pretty hard and figured out there was a slice in time by which we could be in the Gringotts Bank at the moment Harry, Ron, and Hermione were breaking in to steal the Horcrux. It took a lot of thought; it took a lot of consideration to find a way to allow us to be in that moment in the movie, but Gringotts, as you know from the films and books, was a ride waiting to happen. And the chance to bring it to life was an opportunity we just didn't want to miss.

**Mason** — When we laid out Hogsmeade and began all that process, we never realized the crowds. So we needed to be true to the stories, to keep things tight and close, but we also needed to have the space. [In Diagon Alley,] I think we've achieved pretty well this feeling of a tight, closed-in, urban environment, yet to still have the space for our guests.

**Alan Gilmore**, *Supervising Art Director on the Harry Potter films* — The place has been very authentically designed to represent a palace of British architectural history. You're in a medieval building right now [The Leaky Cauldron], which is say, 1,000 years old. You have the Victorian streets, the Victorian architecture that is very typical of London. So I think British people, especially Londoners will warm to this place. They will recognize the train trestle, the train bridge, the sound of the train overhead, all those layers. In our world, back there, it's a very much a layered architecture where buildings are retained, if possible. So we all live in much older structures and there's a real romance to that older structure. We try to enhance that here. Stuart drove a design logic where it's all an enhanced reality, where the buildings lean a little bit more and the colors are a little bit stronger, but it gives that sense of magic.

**David Barron**, *Producer of the Harry Potter films* — Anyone involved in building permanent buildings, they're used to building in straight lines. Yet nothing Stuart designs for these types of sets is straight. [Laughs] It's all off-kilter. Then you have problems with leaky windows, and all kinds of things. You just can't build them in a conventional fashion.

**Gilmore** — [The Three Broomsticks] is one of the most complicated buildings ever constructed in a theme park. All the amazing systems hidden within the shell that you cannot see, all the modern accoutrements, the air conditioning, the electricity, all hidden, you can't see it. We make great efforts to keep you in Harry's world and in an architectural period when things are simple — gas-powered lighting, and very simple decorations. It's all about that immersion.

**Thierry Coup**, *Senior Vice President of Universal Creative* — Fans really love all the details that we put into Hogsmeade and Hogwarts, and the level of storytelling. We wanted to take that and raise the bar one more time and that's what we've done here. We know what the fans love and you come down to Diagon Alley and you can tell this is a whole different level, a whole different scale. We shared a lot of great moments in Hogsmeade and Hogwarts over the past few years with the cast, and we always take their feedback, just like we take the feedback of our guests, and we've applied that to what you see here. We put you into our story.

**Woodbury** — When you think of the cast and the bigger picture of being involved, having a guy like Stuart Craig involved again as our chief production designer on the entire endeavor was really critical. Bringing the entire Harry Potter film franchise back together to help us make this as real and as authentic as possible was really important — to have them as an active part of the process.

**Gilmore** — I think Diagon Alley is utterly beautiful. Coming from the film team, where we only really built Diagon Alley maybe 20 feet high, to have a chance here to build it for real — the roofs, the chimneys, inside the rooms — it's a real, breathing city. To work with these guys and to create this, this scale is so magnificent. To tell all these stories, and the layers of these stories, has been a real joy.

**Coup** — From all the filmmakers, we got the feeling that this was a dream come true for them because when they get to design sets for the films, they are limited to what the camera can see and often there are no ceilings — the "ceilings" are all lights. Yesterday, when the cast came through, they said, 'Wow, there's a sky.' It's great — it's as real as you can make it.

**Mason** — And we get to expand. A movie set is only so big, but we get to take you around the corner, to see what is there, to discover something else.

**Coup** — This allowed us to bring some of the things that were in the books, that you never saw in the films — a lot of details that you needed to read the stories to know about.

**Gilmore** — Even new places, like Horizont Alley. That never existed before, so you've created a new street in London [gesturing toward Coup]. It's all yours.

**Robbie Coltrane**, *Rubeus Hagrid* — The original set [of The Leaky Cauldron], the wall ended about what, at the start of the pictures? [Points to a spot on the wall about 15 feet away.] And now look at that magnificent cathedral ceiling. It's a completely different, with this three-dimensional feel to it. You can go in all the stores. When it's a set, sets have to be moved, so you can put the camera in a different position, or move the lights, or whatever. So they cannot be three-dimensional, whereas here, because it is so permanent, you can wander around all the stores, open the door and go in, and someone will greet you. It's just like being in a real place, weirdly.

**Lewis** — It's so impressive. When we were filming at Leavesden Studios, the sets were brilliant; they were fantastic, but it was very uncommon for us to have a complete set. We'd have half a set, so you can get the cameras in or the crew. Whereas what you've done here, you've created a completely immersive, 3D environment. It's all solid stone. You just can't get this anywhere else. From the moment you're here to the moment you leave, the illusion is never shattered. There's never any electricity cables lying around, you can't see any of the rides when you're in Diagon Alley, you're just in this world, taking this journey. I think if we had filmed the movie here, we'd all have been a lot better. You can't help be get brought into the world.

**Evanna Lynch**, *Luna Lovegood* — I agree. It would have been a lot easier to do the movies [here]. You wouldn't have had to use your imagination so much. Less acting, definitely. [Laughs] I just love that it's totally for the fans. For real fans who know all the details, all the trivia, there are so many details [here] that if you haven't read the books, you could just

DESIGNERS AND ACTORS TALK ABOUT THE WIZARDING WORLD

walk by them and you wouldn't even know. It's just really cool to walk around and you see little details like 'there's where Harry stayed before his third year' [she points to the upstairs of The Leaky Cauldron], and then I'm thinking 'oh yeah, and he wandered up to Florean Fortescue's every day.' You can just walk through the books in this land. You can do a full 360 [degree] turn and you don't see any roller coasters; it's just the skyline, as it should be. I don't think you even need to go on the rides. I just like to wander around and pretend that I'm a witch for a few hours.

**Radcliffe** — Not to be disparaging to film sets, which are incredible, but this world is even more complete. You go out the back of film sets and you see that they are are held together by scaffolding and plaster. Here, there's never a moment when the illusion is broken. I was amazed by it.

**Felton** — I'm still waiting to see a green screen. [Laughter]

**Radcliffe** — For me, the fact that the castle looks as incredible as it does, and it does look about 700-foot high, is kind of amazing, the way it towers over the place. You can hardly fail to be filled with a sense of awe when you see that.

**Domhnall Gleeson**, *Bill Weasley* — I feature in the ride [Gringotts] more than I do in the films, so it was nice to actually see myself. [Laughter] There was a girl last night, using her wand to make stuff work, I think that's where it's at, it's the delight of the people who are in the park, everything about this place is amazing, but when you see the kids doing things, that's when it really comes to life.

**Coltrane** — It's magical. It really is. I'm standing here with a wand like a 10-year-old [waves an imaginary wand].

**Gleeson** — I couldn't do it for a while! [They laugh] I had to perfect it.

**Bonnie Wright**, *Ginny Weasley* — There's so much history behind [Diagon Alley], which is, all the things that Jo Rowling wrote in the books that unfortunately we didn't get to explain every tiny little detail in the films — all those extra details that she put into the books, the backstory, — for fans who really did, with a fine-toothed comb, learn her story and her world, will get to see it here.

**Dave Cobb**, *Senior Creative Director at Thinkwell Group* — Here's a story: I'm drinking my Butterbeer, walking around, enjoying the sites. I walk behind the The Three Broomsticks and I see a group of about eight or 10 14-year-olds, in full school robes. They were far too young to work there, but then I looked at what they were doing. Spread out on the table in front of them is their homework. From school. They are *cosplaying their homework*. [Laughter] So I walk up and ask them, and they're like, 'Yeah, we come here three days a week. We go to Dr. Phillips High School, behind the park. We have season passes. Our parents drop us off. We finish our homework, have a Butterbeer, ride the ride, and go home.' Three days a week. Did Universal plan on having school groups do homework in the park? No! And they're in full Hogwarts robes. So, those kids are using that space in a way that was completely unintended. Places become their own reason for being, and the audience will use your place for their own purposes.

**Woodbury** — Somebody asked earlier about what we'd learned during the process of Hogsmeade to now. One of those things that we did learn, and Thierry touched on it before, was that people enjoy the discovery and exploration part of this experience more than any particular ride or individual thing. It's kind of 'sum of the parts' experience. So we really focused on that. If you look at the wardrobe, and you look at the interactions with the characters that inhabit these places, we focused a lot of time on trying to make that a seamless, immersive part of the whole journey through Diagon Alley.

**Helena Bonham Carter**, *Bellatrix Lestrange* — It really has created a sense of wonder — real wonder, and enchantment. It's transporting. But you see, for the kids, I think they're more naturally in that state anyway. It doesn't take much for them to be transported because their imaginations are so much more available. Somewhere, we tend to close down. Well, some of use do. As actors, we're just paid to imagine. But what's so great about this, is it's better than what we had to act in. We didn't have ceilings. Look at that ceiling. We didn't have a ceiling; it would just stop at about 10 feet. And sometimes, we didn't have anything. It's just... green. Green, green, green, green — and that was it. My first scene, actually, it was completely empty — there was nothing. It's really weird. You have one huge, empty space. There's nothing to relate to. In a weird way, you can get a kind of vertigo when it's all green. It was hard. So when you get this three dimensional set, it just does most of the imagining for you.

**Felton** — I remember we had some children visiting the sets most days and a lot of them were underwhelmed with the big green screen. [Laughter] Watching us play Quidditch was never as exciting as it came out on the film. So it's great for them to get a chance to come now and see it for real.

**Radcliffe** — It's that little noise that kids make — "ahh!" — and if you could bottle it, that's the reason this park exists. It's fantastic.

**Felton** — It's nice for us [too]. They're keeping the candle alive, really, aren't they? I've said that if I ever get withdrawal symptoms, I can just come back here and revel in it.

**Gleeson** — I think the whole thing was special for me. It's amazing to think that so many different people are going to go on those rides and, hopefully, have a brilliant time. It's very nice to think that we have been a part of that.

**Barron** — We're sitting in the legacy, really, that will be left when the films are gone and there are no more books to be published. This is what will be left, and what it is the tangible manifestation of what we present as a fantasy on film. You can live and breathe the world in a complete fashion here.

*The Cabana Bay Beach Resort opened in 2014, one of the four on-site hotels at the Universal Orlando Resort.*

# TIPS FOR VISITING THE WIZARDING WORLD AND UNIVERSAL ORLANDO RESORT

As we've mentioned, The Wizarding World of Harry Potter is part of the Universal Orlando Resort. So you'll need Universal Orlando theme park tickets to get into the two lands. If you are not familiar with the resort, Universal Orlando includes two theme parks — Universal Studios Florida and Islands of Adventure — as well as four on-site hotels, and a shopping-and-dining area called CityWalk.

An Islands of Adventure ticket includes admission to Hogsmeade, as well as the other lands in the park, including attractions devoted to Jurassic Park, Dr. Seuss, and Marvel. (Yes, Disney owns Marvel now, but before Disney bought the comic-book company, Marvel sold its Orlando-area theme parks rights to Universal in perpetuity. That's why you will not see the classic Marvel characters, including Spider-Man and the Incredible Hulk, inside the Walt Disney World theme parks. But you will see them here.)

A ticket to Universal Studios Florida gets you into Diagon Alley, as well as that park's other lands, which include attractions themed to The Simpsons, Transformers, and Men in Black. But if you want to ride the Hogwarts Express between the two parks, you will need to buy a Park-to-Park ticket, rather than a ticket that's good for only one theme park per day. Keep that in mind when pricing tickets for your vacation.

As with all the Orlando-area theme parks, crowds are at their largest during the school vacations, especially late May to mid-August, the week of Thanksgiving in late November, and the weeks around Christmas and New Year's Day. Universal's "Mardi Gras" concert series also attracts people to the park during late winter to mid-spring. And you'll find reduced hours at Universal Studios Florida in late September through October due to the after-hours, extra-ticket-required "Halloween Horror Nights" event that runs during that time of year.

If you've got some flexibility in your vacation schedule, the best times to visit Universal Orlando to avoid big crowds are late August through mid-September, early November, early December, non-holiday weeks in January and February, and then late April through mid-May.

If you're a big Potter fan and want to share the parks with a huge crowd of other Potter fans, consider visiting during Universal's annual "Celebration of Harry Potter" weekend, usually in late January. The weekend event includes appearance by supporting-cast actors from the Harry Potter films, question-and-answer sessions, special exhibitions of movie props and costumes, and special merchandise sales. The whole affair is open to all park ticket-holders, but Universal sells special hotel vacation packages for the weekend that include reserved admission and seating to the various events.

If you can afford it, staying at one of Universal Orlando's on-site hotels provides you extra access to The Wizarding World of Harry Potter lands, which also can help you avoid spending hours of your visit waiting in lines. Guests at all four Universal hotels get one hour of early access to at least one of the Wizarding World lands before it opens to the public each day. In addition, guests at Universal's Portofino Bay Resort, Hard Rock Hotel, and Royal Pacific Resort get unlimited front-of-the-line "Universal Express" access to almost all attractions in both theme parks.

The Universal Express deal might be one of the great perks in the vacation industry — it changes completely the way that a family can approach its theme park visit. No longer do you have to worry about getting to the park at the right time, or in which order to go on what rides. With front-of-the-line access to almost everything, you just go on what you want, when you want. The benefit starts on the day you check in and ends on the day you check out, so just one night in one of the "top three" Universal Orlando hotels allows you two days of front-of-line access.

You might have noticed that I keep writing "almost everything." Universal Express access does not apply to three rides: "Harry Potter and the Forbidden Journey," "Harry Potter and the Escape from Gringotts," and "Pteranodon Flyers" — a low-capacity kids' ride in the Jurassic Park section of Islands of Adventure. But your hotel stay does qualify you for early access to the two Harry Potter rides, so start your days there. Arrive for the early entry before it begins, so you can be among the first in line for Forbidden Journey or Gringotts. Do one of those rides first, then enjoy the rest of the land before going out into the rest of the parks, where you will have front-of-line access. Also remember that as an early entrant, you can be first in line to ride the Hogwarts Express over to the other park, allowing you a bit of a jump into the queues over there, as it will take other visitors several minutes to walk through the park after it opens.

If you are not staying on-site at Universal Orlando, you still should try to arrive before the parks open, then make your way straight back to the Harry Potter land in the park you're visiting. Even though Universal hotel guests will be in the lands early, the crowds in the morning still will be smaller than later in the day. Look on the UniversalOrlando.com website for park schedules, to see if on-site hotel guests are limited to one of the two Wizarding Worlds for early entry. If so, start your day at the other Wizarding World for the shortest possible wait over there.

Forbidden Journey and Gringotts also offer single-rider queues that might allow you a significantly shorter wait time than going through the traditional queue. If you're traveling alone, or willing to split your party to take advantage of a shorter wait, ask about the single-rider line at the attraction entrance. Keep in mind that the single-rider line might not always be available. If they back up too much, Universal will close access to them, and the parks won't offer them on slower days, either. Elsewhere in the parks, time-saving single-rider queues are available on The Amazing Adventures of Spider-Man, Doctor Doom's Fearfall, Incredible Hulk Coaster, Dudley Do-Right's Ripsaw Falls, and the Jurassic Park River Adventure in Islands of Adventure, and on Transformers: The Ride 3D, Despicable Me Minion Mayhem, Hollywood Rip Ride Rockit, Revenge of the Mummy, and Men in Black: Alien Attack in Universal Studios Florida.

During the first summer of operation for Gringotts, Universal was cutting access to the ride an hour or two before the park closed, to provide extra time for maintenance work in the evenings. That might change in the months to come, but to be certain that you get to ride, don't plan to wait until the evening to ride Gringotts for the first time.

If you aren't into thrill rides, but want to see the impressive sights within Hogwarts Castle and Gringotts Bank, you can "take the tour" and go through the queue, then bail on the taking the ride. Just tell the team member at the load station that you want to skip the ride. That's just after you see the sorting hat in Forbidden Journey and when you pick up the 3D glasses after the elevator ride in Gringotts.

If you are a American Automobile Association member, you can get a discount on admission, food, and merchandise at many locations throughout Universal Orlando by showing your AAA membership card.

If you are visiting from outside the United States, please note that posted prices in America do not include sales taxes, which will be added to your charges when you pay. Also remember that waiters in table-service restaurants should be tipped 15-20% of the bill, as almost all of their pay is from customer tips.

If you decide to exchange your Muggle money for Gringotts Bank Notes at the currency exchange in Diagon Alley, that "wizard money" can be used at shops and restaurants throughout the Universal Orlando Resort, and not just within the two Wizarding World lands. So don't make a long walk back to the currency exchange if you have some Gringotts notes left over after your stay in Diagon Alley or Hogsmeade. You can spend them or exchange them back into U.S. dollars elsewhere around the resort.

On the flip side of that advice, if you forget to buy a Potter-themed souvenir you'd had your eye on inside the Wizarding World, Universal Orlando sells its Harry Potter merchandise online at *https://www.universalorlando.com/Merchandise/Shop/Harry_Potter.html*

If you did buy your souvenirs in the park and you are staying on-site at Universal Orlando, you can have your purchases delivered to your hotel room at no extra charge, saving you the hassle of carrying them around the park all day.

If you would like more tips on planning an Orlando-area theme park vacation, please pick up the latest edition of *Theme Park Insider Visits Walt Disney World and Universal Orlando*, our complete guidebook to all the attractions, restaurants, and hotels at the Universal Orlando and Walt Disney World Resorts.

*Harry Potter merchandise for sale at the Warner Bros. VIP Studio Tour in Los Angeles*

# THE WIZARDING WORLD BEYOND ORLANDO

In 2012, before Universal confirmed plans for a second Harry Potter land at Universal Orlando, the company confirmed that it would bring the Wizarding World of Harry Potter to **Universal Studios Japan** in Osaka. The Japanese Wizarding World debuted on July 15, 2014, one week after the opening of Diagon Alley in Orlando.

Osaka's Wizarding World is based on the Hogsmeade Village design from Islands of Adventure, with just a few tweaks. There's no Dragon Challenge roller coaster in the Osaka version of the land. And, with no Diagon Alley to connect with, there's no Hogwarts Express ride, either, though there is a stationary Hogwarts Express locomotive as a photo opportunity. But the land retains the Zonko's Joke Shop that was removed in Orlando. The rest of the land includes Honeydukes, The Three Broomsticks, the Hog's Head Pub, Ollivander's, Dervish and Banges, Flich's Emporium of Confiscated Goods, the "Flying Hippogriff," and "Harry Potter and the Forbidden Journey."

(A bit of trivia for you — at Universal Studios Japan, The Wizarding World of Harry Potter is located just behind the Jaws attraction, the ride that Diagon Alley replaced in Orlando.)

The Southern California version of the Wizarding World was the first to be announced following the opening of the original Wizarding World in Orlando, but it will be the last to be completed, with a 2016 opening planned. **Universal Studios Hollywood** is building Hollywood's Hogwarts Castle on the site of the now-demolished Gibson (*nee* Universal) Amphitheater, as part of a $1.6 billion "Evolution" revitalization plan for the Hollywood theme park and production studio property.

The Wizarding World of Harry Potter at Universal Studios Hollywood also will follow the Hogsmeade Village design, though Universal has not yet officially announced the line-up of shops and attractions for this version of the land. However, we expect to see a similar line-up as in Japan — with a Forbidden Journey ride in the castle, The Three Broomsticks restaurant in the village... and no Dragon Challenge coaster.

Harry Potter fans in Southern California don't have to wait until 2016 to experience a bit of the Wizarding World in their hometown. Remember that Universal developed its Harry Potter attractions under license from Warner Bros., the movie studio that distributed the Harry Potter films. Warner Bros.' main studio lot lies just down the road from Universal Studios Hollywood — it fact, you can see it from the "Starway" escalators that connect the upper and lower lots of the Universal Studios Hollywood theme park.

Even though Warner Bros. did not build a theme park around its movie studio, it does offer studio tours to the public. And those tours include a healthy dose of Potter. Harry Potter merchandise — including house robes, T-shirts, and wands — are available for sale in the gift shop where the **Warner Bros. VIP Studio Tours** begin and end. You can get even get Every-Flavor Beans and Chocolate Frogs! But there's no Butterbeer, alas. The real highlight for Potter fans is the Studio Archives at the end of the tour, where fans can see authentic props and costumes from the Harry Potter films. The tour lasts about two hours and is open to visitors ages 8 and older. Tickets must be purchased in advance and are available online at *http://vipstudiotour.warnerbros.com.*

Something you won't see on that tour, though, is any of the sets or stages where the Potter movies were filmed. That all happened at the Leavesden Studios in England. However, if you are in the United Kingdom, Warner Bros. has opened a Harry Potter-themed tour of those studios. The **Warner Bros. Studio Tour London** opened March 31, 2012 and features a look inside two of the sound stages where the movies were filmed, as well as a tour through the studio's backlot, where many of the sets, props and costumes from the eight films have been preserved for fans to see. At Leavesden, you can see for yourself what Robbie Coltrane and other Harry Potter cast members were talking about at the Diagon Alley opening, when they compared Universal Orlando's land to the sets where they'd worked. Plus, this is the only place outside the Universal theme parks where you can buy an official Butterbeer. The tour lasts about three and a half hours and is open to all ages. Tickets must be purchased in advance and are available online at *http://www.wbstudiotour.co.uk.*

So what's next in the Wizarding World? When Universal Orlando's creative team was asked about future Harry Potter projects, they evaded the question. So at least we know that no one in the know is *denying* that a new Wizarding World land might be built!

Several Diagon Alley visitors have noted how one side of the new land just seems to trail off into a dead end. Carkitt Market seems to be leading somewhere, but doesn't. On the London facade side at that same point, we see Grimmauld Place curving around the London waterfront and just... ending. It seems an odd way to end a land that's so full of exclamation points.

Diagon Alley's neighbor on that side in Universal Studios Florida is the "Fear Factor Live" stage, where park visitors participate in a live version of a TV reality show that Universal's corporate sibling NBC cancelled years ago. "Fear Factor Live" doesn't even run during the slower times of the year in the park. It's long been considered an obvious candidate for replacement. Put two and two together, and the design of Diagon Alley makes more sense if you see it as just the beginning of Harry Potter's London in Universal Studios Florida. Imagine the London facade continuing around the park's central lagoon, into the space now occupied by "Fear Factor Live." And behind that facade, imagine an extension of Diagon Alley that would include the Ministry of Magic. Fans have been buzzing about the possibility for years now, as rumors about a third, and even a fourth, Harry Potter land at Universal Orlando resort won't fade away.

A fourth Harry Potter land? With *Fantastic Beasts and Where to Find Them* scheduled to hit movie theaters in 2016, interest in the Wizarding World's magical creatures soon might be stoked even higher. Universal cleaved Hogsmeade from its Lost Continent land in Islands of Adventure, leaving two shows and a restaurant behind. What if Universal finished the job, and converted the rest of Lost Continent to a Harry Potter theme, creating a Forbidden Forest extension to Hogsmeade?

As we mentioned at the start of the book, Harry Potter has been very, very good to NBCUniversal, driving the company's theme parks to record attendance, revenue, and profits. If movie studios won't stop making sequels to wildly successful films, it's hard to imagine that Universal Studios wouldn't want to continue developing its Wizarding Worlds, to provide Potter fans with fresh new reasons to come — and keeping coming back — to the Universal Orlando Resort.

No matter what happens at Universal Orlando and the other Universal theme parks around the world, we will be there to cover it. So, please, keep visiting us online at ThemeParkInsider.com for all the latest news from The Wizarding World of Harry Potter, in Orlando and beyond.

# ABOUT THE AUTHOR

Robert Niles is the founder and editor of ThemeParkInsider.com, an online consumers' guide to the world's leading theme and amusement parks, read by more than 300,000 people each month. It has been named the top theme park site on the Internet by *Forbes* and *Travel + Leisure* magazines, has been a Webby Award finalist, and is a winner of the prestigious Online Journalism Award, presented then by the Online News Association and the Columbia Graduate School of Journalism.

Robert worked at Walt Disney World's Magic Kingdom for five summers between 1987 and 1991, as well as for a full year between graduating Northwestern University and beginning graduate school in journalism at another university. In the years since leaving Disney, Robert has worked as a reporter, editorial writer, columnist, and website editor for several newspapers, including *The* [Bloomington, Indiana] *Herald-Times*, the *Omaha* [Nebraska] *World-Herald*, the [Denver] *Rocky Mountain News* and the *Los Angeles Times*.

Robert is a native of Los Angeles and today lives in Pasadena, California.

You can follow ThemeParkInsider.com on the Internet at *http://www.themeparkinsider.com*.

We're also on Facebook at *http://www.facebook.com/themeparkinsider*.

And Twitter at *http://twitter.com/themepark*.

Made in the USA
Lexington, KY
06 October 2015